The Lost Hare

Poetry by Nina Bogin

In the North
The Winter Orchards

Nina Bogin

The Lost Hare

ANVIL PRESS POETRY

Published in 2012
by Anvil Press Poetry Ltd
' Neptune House 70 Royal Hill London SE10 8RF
www.anvilpresspoetry.com

Copyright © Nina Bogin 2012

This book is published with financial assistance
from Arts Council England

Designed and set in Monotype Ehrhardt by Anvil
Printed and bound in Great Britain
by Hobbs the Printers Ltd

ISBN 978 0 85646 445 4

A catalogue record for this book
is available from the British Library

for Alain

ACKNOWLEDGEMENTS

Some of the poems in this collection have
appeared in the following magazines:

Ambit: A Wheatfield; The Old World
Cairn: The Wayfarers
Little Star: The Lost Hare; The Blue Threshold
PN Review: The Divorce; You
The Times Literary Supplement:
    from A Portfolio: Homework; School Door
    from Poems of France: Blackthorn; Bunker,
Champagney; Small Factory; Musk Mallow

The title 'The Blue Threshold' (*Blaue Schwelle*)
was taken from a series of paintings by the Swiss
painter Franziska Gloor.

The epigraph is taken from *Darkness Spoken, The
Collected Poems of Ingeborg Bachmann* (Zephyr
Press, 2006) translated by Peter Filkins.

CONTENTS

Liegt Böhmen noch am Meer, glaub ich den Meeren wieder.
Und glaub ich noch ans Meer, so hoffe ich auf Land.

If Bohemia lies by the sea, I'll believe in the sea again.
And believing in the sea, I can hope for land.

Ingeborg Bachmann, from *Böhmen liegt am Meer*
(*Bohemia Lies by the Sea*)

MEASUREMENT

Close to the ground
where the world begins.
Pockets of rainwater, stones.
Grass new and upright.
A snail on its silver track.
And over it all, millions
of compass-points of light,
generous, exact,
apportioning to each of us
one measure of sobriety,
one of delight.

THE WAYFARERS

In those nineteenth-century engravings
of landscapes etched deep with rocks
and torrents, towering pines
and vertiginous slopes,

on a promontory
jutting into the turbulent sky,
two men stand in city clothes
discoursing on progress and hope;

one leans on a walking stick,
the other peers through a telescope;
both gesture upwards, where an eagle
circles in the stir,

invitation or warning,
or both. For the moment,
stalwart as they are,
they're dwarfed

by the pinnacles above them;
nature is a forbidding place.
Whom can they turn to but themselves?
There is a way out of here,

though, that narrow path
chiseled into the cliff
that takes the middle course
between forest gloom

and heady peaks; it leads
to a tableland of green, neither too high
nor too low, where a farm
nestles in the combe; it's there

the wayfarers will bend their step
for, beyond the etching's wooden frame,
the town is not far off
to which all roads return.

For we cannot expect these heroes
to spend all their breath
on the open air; science awaits them.
They'll find an inn

where, after soup and bread,
they'll feast on stewed hare
washed down with an old wine,
and long into the night

around the oaken table
they'll speak of destiny
and how they'll carve
the future

with their own keen sense
of purpose and clairvoyance.
Or so they believed.
Let us leave them there,

smoking their pipes
as the fire burns low
in the grate, the candles
flickering on the mantelpiece

and the warmth shuttered in;
without, the river rushes past
the gabled houses, the stars
gleam for owl and fox,

and we, years from being born,
will wake to what they,
in their ignorance,
fashioned.

ELEGY

for Allan

After you died in your forties,
I thought about your parents' home
and the parties you threw
when we were a slew of sophisticated teens
listening to Shostakovich and the Rolling Stones,
future artists, most of us – writers, musicians, dancers
    like you –
talented, handsome, fey, a gracious host
ushering us into the living room, elegant and dark
with porcelains and scrolls brought back from the Orient.
Your doctor parents were never in,
leaving us to be Dionysian and intense,
making a mess someone else cleaned up.
All evening, while Mick Jagger wailed
and couples smoked and danced,
a ferocious dog, locked in the basement,
lunged and lunged against the kitchen door.

One night your rarely-mentioned elder brother –
escaped from a clinic –
threw himself under a train.
Overnight you were older than we would be for years,
impassive, contained.
It was the year of Zeffirelli's "Romeo and Juliet".
We drove into the city on a Friday night,
three boys and me, sat in the back of the movie theatre
and sank, the four of us together,
into the film's romantic, adolescent dream.
When it ended, with hopeless love and beauty dead,

we sat there stunned. Without a word
we left the theater, without a word
we drove back home, amazed
at our capacity for silence at that early age,
our grief for you locked up inside the car.

THE LOST HARE

Every day a different weather,
weeks without seeing moon or sun,
and a hare I've been trying to track down
these twelve years gone, ever since

I glimpsed it, deep in thought,
in the high grass of the marsh;
I saw the ash-grey tips of its ears.
Seeing me, it disappeared

into blackthorn and wild rose,
leaving its burrows unattended,
the entryways clogging with cobwebs.
In the meantime

my hair has gone grey,
my hands thick-veined, and the lines
of my thwarted quest cross my face
from every direction.

My long-haired daughters have grown,
left for other cities. We tend the fire,
keep the rooms clean, lay the table for two.
And beyond the black door

the sky fills up with stars
shedding their slow light
on the innumerable paths
through the marsh-grass

to the hollow
where the lost hare sleeps
bedded down in the thoughts
and dreams I hoarded there.

THE OLD WORLD

These towns, these places on the map,
come complete with auras, their names
resounding like chimes. Rivers and bridges,
steeples and the smell of ink.
I look down from the bell-towers
and see them spiraled at my feet:
the vendors in the square, the cobbled streets
where the first editions were churned out,
rainwater flowing through the gutters to the sea.

Flocks of starlings fly up and up, winding me
into their legend, who once toiled in the fields
or, in the back alleys, scrubbed blackened pots and pans,
never learned to read, and long ago
disappeared into an abandoned grave
where the Hebrew letters of my name blend
into the moss-covered stone of the land.

YOUR WORDS

Your words trouble the silver twilight.
Mid-winter, and we are all alive.

But the mountains have moved closer,
their violet folds like a shawl

we might wrap around us
to keep out the cold.

A first star appears, and immediately
I'm drawn to it like a charm.

If I care hard enough, as the sky deepens
into a fragile, indigo calm,

perhaps it will keep us from harm.
But tonight I can't be fooled.

All day, I've carried your bad news
like a stone in my pocket

I keep fingering
with my gloves on.

A HOMECOMING

I

We never learned to drive a sleigh, to slap the reins
on the backs of four white horses
and gallop into the sky

but drunk on brightness and cold,
we sledded down slopes
of newly fallen snow

when did I cease to see your face
behind the drifts of years
that blurred your leave-taking?

II

We were born after the war
but the war was inside us

it followed us into the schoolyard
under the trees, I remember

a girl telling about the camps, the atrocities,
she swore it was true

in our school on Long Island
of mostly Jewish children

you were the German boy
the kids called Nazi

the war accompanied us
through our childhoods

it stayed with some of us more than others
we learned to live with it

but in you it went on warring
until it had broken your family

your mother, your father, your sisters,
until it had broken you

and thrown you helter-skelter
across the years and continents

until at last you stopped,
drew out from your heart

the shards of ice,
and began your own life.

III

At cross-purposes,
a give-and-take.
While you were falling,
I was rising.
While you wandered,
I staked my claim.
While you flung angry words
like prehistoric stones,
I strove to sweeten my rage
like honeycomb.
You fled from women,
I became a wife.
You fathered sons,
I mothered daughters.
You wavered,
I held my own.
You argued,
I complied.
You stood outside,
I stayed within.
Flip sides of a coin.
Assonance and dissonance.
We take the measure
of the distance between us.

IV

In the end there were no snowy meadows,
no forests to fell,
no rivers to cross,

and the horses had long since
been unyoked and bedded down in straw,
the sleighs upended and forgotten.

But whatever we were
left a trace that we, sleep-walkers,
daydreamers, followed,

our footsteps falling into place
on an invisible path that led us
through thick and thin

to a homecoming
far from home,
in a stark November light

that lit us from within,
as if we could illuminate
this story of our lives.

WINTER SOLSTICE

The solstice draws its net
over the blue hillside,
the low stars.

So I return to early things,
my love of moss, the pungent
under-sides of firs.

I listen to the deepening of shadows,
the wind steeped in indigo.
Here under the hill

I am small as an acorn
with its one hard truth.
Night falls. I dig in

my heels, feel
seeds settle, the earth
grow still.

DECEMBER

I love this scant blue light
running low across hard grass

to the end of the year as though
there might not be a next

these slivers of sky
glancing off the sharp edge of winter

I too splinter in all directions
I run to catch up with myself

I drink in the plum-colored dusk
it goes straight to my head

I want these slanting hours to last
so I can take my time

to enter their darkness
and hold their blue incandescence

inside me like a word
old as starlight.

SNOW WATER

The brook runs narrow with snow-water
cutting an urgent passage through the woods

the air is rich with the odor of earth
the water rushes clear and brown

over stones, tree-roots, fallen branches,
copper-colored leaves

yellow grass under bulbs of ice,
every size and shape of seeds

gathering in dark eddies, waiting for the surge
of impatient water to move them along

because everything that has been given
will be carried away

and my memories floating
on the reflection of the sky

grey and blue, wisps of clouds
riding gently on the surface

our lives move onward
if we can only accept the flow

my hands in the snow-water
ice-cold earth-colored

running between my fingers
there is nothing to hold onto

and nothing holds onto us
but ourselves

A WHEATFIELD

Our bodies are the color of wheat, in a field
alongside a river, where long-necked geese
spread out over the marshes, their wings carrying them
on spirals of wind. We too skimmed across
the world as we held each other, our skin sweet
with the scent of grass, warm from the sun that flooded
our mornings. And below us were the same green banks
tangled with violets and cowslips, the purple spikes of
    milkwort
that brought us, year in, year out, our awaited springs.
It can't be true that each day we are new, for each day
we are older, but we keep more and lose less,
and all the things we took no heed of – how fallen oak
    leaves
place themselves on beds of moss, how your body
marries the slope of mine – are as clear now as when
we first lay flank to flank and let ourselves be borne
to river-marshes, where wheat rippled in the sun,
where the geese tilted their long grey necks like rudders
and hoisted themselves into one blue V, honking
and calling as they spun out before us.

YOU

Twenty-five years.
Others have come to take
your place, to wear the clothes
you might have worn, to speak
the words that would have been
your birth-right. Your hair might
have fallen across your forehead
like theirs, you might
have turned halfway, your face
lit by firelight. Your eyes
would have been thoughtful
by now, with thoughts we could
guess knowing your habits and
desires, we would have warmed
to the honey of your voice, harkened
to your footfall on the stairs.
In your long black coat, your pockets
weighed down by your preferred
philosophers, you would have wrapped
your arms around a cherished woman,
buried your face in her hair, breathed in
her cinnamon scent. You would be
here with all the certainty of your
twenty-five years, tall and forthright
in the dark-enfolding night,
first-born, stillborn son,
passing by on the far side of life.

BEARINGS

I'm trying to get my bearings
in this landscape of green

at every turn I stumble upon
trees, bushes, hedges

summer unsettles me,
all the boundaries are blurred

between the earth and the sky,
the days and the nights

so I can't remember anything
useful or significant

like the phases of the moon
or the position of Orion

I don't know if it's a beginning
or an end, a coming-together

or a taking-away, all these leaves
and stems, these tendrils choking the life

out of each other, sweet pea,
morning glory, with their reckless

flowers spilling every which way,
all the tender words I've stored up for you

as I make my way
unguided

through the world

ONCE

Once my mother's arms
were a kingdom around me.

Softly rocked, I nestled
in the velvet of her lap,

waking drowsy, confident,
rosy-cheeked.

But I had a stubborn,
independent streak.

I wanted to be only
I, to fashion myself

from my own rib.
Unloosened

from those gentle bonds,
I flew away, little grey dove

heady with daring,
bold in love.

I know I was proud,
shaped, perhaps,

by a mistaken mold,
even if the contours of a life

are blurred, imprecise –
more chance than choice

when all is said and done.
Now, when she's gone,

it's her gaze I recognize
as in the mirror it meets mine:

the steady hazel eyes, thick eyebrows,
the inquisitive regard –

our questions and answers
left unsaid.

THE HAWK

Everyone knows the hawk.
He's a switch-blade, stainless-steel.

Flicked open,
he scours the air

with a metal whirr
that sets your teeth on edge.

You feel
the cold span of his wing

like a guillotine
above your head.

Then, snapped shut,
he sits on a branch.

Broods. Peers out
from under his hood.

Nursing an old grievance,
his feathers splayed

in disarray,
he bides his time.

It's the fault
of every little creature

too small to sate his hunger
that he must spend his days

in trees, on fence-posts
scouting for sparrows, field mice, snakes.

Unsung henchman
with no kingdom

to defend, it's not he
but the world that's wrong.

Oblivious
to all the passing centuries,

he wreaks his revenge.

UNDER ORION

I live by a night-blue forest,
thick with the gutturals
of hawks and jays, crows and owls.
Here, as everywhere, the moon
waxes and wanes, and across the black sky
Orion makes his rounds.

But the language I speak
has lost its home.
Inside the words I use
are words I've forgotten,
buried dialects, whole alphabets
left on the far side of rivers.

I feel them crowding my mouth,
adding their weight
to what I have no words for.
They are the grit in my teeth,
the slow Slavic song
that rolls off my tongue.

And in my eyes, somewhere between
the hazel and green of the marshlands
of the Danube, a question
drifting through the reeds
reaches me after all these years:
why are you not here?

Here is the language I married
without taking its name,
qui m'est si proche,

here is where you are, and owls and crows,
where Orion, his sword at his side,
straddles the sky over my house.

There is my fatherland,
my mother tongue.
To those who crossed borders,
who entered its harbors,
I ask forgiveness. I had no excuse,
only my desire

and a star,
a constellation that's watched over
the cities I've lived in,
the landscapes I've loved,
Orion whom I followed, faithful as Sirius –
or who followed me.

Tell me then, Orion,
where can I place the four poles
of my language, while you
pace my land?
Who will hear me
through the blur of these lost tongues?

GLOBEFLOWERS

For you these
apricot-colored globeflowers
in a glass vase

for your golden hair, Reinhilde,
in the Venetian afternoon

like a Rhenish madonna
you walked down the Zattere
in a sweeping lavender dress

arm in arm with your fiancé,
your hair like a cape

the years waver
like golden globeflowers
on their stems

I keep looking for you,
Reinhilde

and your grey Flemish eyes,
your whispered voice,
your apricot hair

in the water-blue afternoon
mirrored in canal after canal

there's no sign of you
in Venice or in Antwerp,
in Bologna or in Bruges

so tonight I'll light a candle for you,
too late or too soon

it will flicker among the globeflowers
and warm my fingers
as I write this poem

for you, Reinhilde,
and the candelabra of your hair.

A PORTFOLIO

Nine photographs of Ingeborg Bachmann
Klagenfurt 1926–Rome 1973

Homework

You're bent over a schoolbook, your bowl-cut hair
hiding your face. Stockings and shoes,
a long-sleeved Tyrolean dress. Nothing matters –

not the bench you're half-sitting on,
nor the photographer you're feigning to ignore,
nor the spring afternoon and its stark light.

There's only the wide-open book
you're leaning on with all your weight,
a pen in your hand

and the word you are about to write.

Bicycle

Both of you are smiling:
daughter in skirt, father in lederhosen.

Straddling the bicycle rack
while he pedals,

you beam at the camera,
eager to please.

Behind you, the green
meadow of your insouciance.

Ahead, the road that will take you
farther and farther away from it.

Dresses

You stand in your frilly peacetime dresses
alongside Jack, the Austrian-Jewish soldier
in British uniform. His arm's looped over

another girl's shoulder. But it's you he knows.
To him – first friend, first confidant –
you've bared your soul.

Now the air is heavy with impossible equations:
three young women, one soldier. Perhaps
that's why you're looking sideways

with a wide, unblinking gaze, as if
like the summer breeze ruffling your skirt,
you're already on your way out of the picture.

Lipstick

Your red, red lips.
They've tasted

the rich wines of desire, love.
You're the poet

up from Carinthia
who's already undone

Vienna's literary men,
taken your place at the table,

filled your glass to the brim.
You lean towards him –

the other poet,
the *ausländer* –

intent, unsure of your charm,
the words between you

a fugue for two voices,
no one's rose, in the storm of roses.

Your heavy lips
that welcome him,

his careful gaze
that strokes your skin.

How brave your lips are!
Saying two things at the same time:

Come into the chambers of my heart.
Come in, but do me no harm.

Chess Game

Your face is a mask, soft and demure
as a cat. You bend over the chessboard,

ready to pounce.
A visit from your brother,

an evening at your flat.
His presence soothes you,

you almost purr.
Via de Notaris, Rome.

This is the city you love,
where you've made your home.

You've chosen the place, the man,
the life. If not happiness,

may courage suffice!
You move your pawn.

Necklace

You don't look at the camera, you rarely do.
In your elegant sheath, you cross your legs.
The ash from your cigarette falls to the floor.

Your hair brushes across your cheek.
These days you look younger, sleek.
A string of pearls adorns your neck.

But this is just the veneer.
Inside, over a wound that will never heal,
you are forging words of steel.

School Door

Your high school's door is too heavy for you. You've been ill.
The perfume of clinics and bed–sheets clings to your hair.
Your grip's gone slack.

But you're out in the sun, drawing in its warmth.
You look ahead. One step after the other.
Your hand on the latch, you hold on for dear life.

Cigarette

The ubiquitous cigarette
between your fingers.

The tumbler of whiskey.
The sleeping pill.

The bleak triumvirate
of your pain

like a black umbrella,
its spokes askew.

When you woke at last
to the flames,

death –
that ultimate art –

had already found
a way out for you.

Epilogue

Rain gear. A stormy beach,
perhaps, by the sea.
You face into the wind.

Your wide smile,
your wet hair.
You're at the far reaches

of Bohemia, perhaps,
your chosen land,
by the sea.

SHE WOLF

In these feral times
I'll be a she-wolf again.
My yellow eyes will gleam.

No one likes me?
I'll bare my teeth
jagged as a bread-knife.

I'll be an outcast,
a stranger in this hinterland
I prowl.

Across the tundra
of backyards and bushes
I'll track the lost scents

of my ancestors,
claim their territory
as my own.

And I'll walk
in my own footprints
even if I fool no one.

THE DIVORCE

From this point onward, everything will go backward.
The rugs will slide out from under their feet.
The lamps will click off, one after the other,
as the doors to each room are opened, then shut.
The last teacups will huddle on the sideboard.

Pried from their fingers, the gold rings
will roll across the polished floors
and lose themselves in little clumps of dust
under the carved oak armoires
emptied of all their belongings.

Blackthorn

Nobody considers blackthorn a flower
until, trailing for miles along rail-lines
and field-ends, it suddenly bursts

into bloom. White fists of petals,
outsized thorns. Like barbed wire
left to its own devices,

it twists and turns
through this no-man's-land
and all its interstices.

Stations

From Paris to Basel
along the old railroad line,
one field still leads to another.

Then cities appear, a maze
of jumbled roofs and grey facades.
Cracked platforms. Faded signs.

Even their names are vestiges –
Troyes, Chaumont, Vesoul.
Their proud stones crumble,

not to be raised again.

Bunker, Champagney

Nothing can wear down a bunker,
not time nor weather
nor indifference nor disgrace.

Its ghosts slipped away long ago –
nameless soldiers of the Wehrmacht,
their canteens and helmets turned to rust.

It's no worse now than any other
out-of-the-way eyesore –
a block of concrete adrift in weeds.

But spoiling in its trapped air
are dark spores of evil.
Trespassers, beware.

Border Post, Ottmarsheim

Yellow flowers grow here now.
Saxifrage splits the pavement,
dandelions' tasseled crowns

reign over the unused lanes
of the empty customs bureaus
where, coming and going,

roadblocks slow us down
though there's no one to wave us through.
Willkommen in Deutschland.

Bienvenue en France.
The Rhine, sluggish between factories,
heaves its way north.

Roots sunk deep in the asphalt,
the yellow flowers hold their ground,
the milk of their stems

drop by drop
replenishing the worn-out land.

War Monuments

There's one for each village, each town,
sculpted in the local stone –
marble, granite, pink sandstone.

Carved in the stone
over plantings of geraniums
are the names of the men

who died for honor,
who died for nothing
at Chemin des Dames,

Ypres, Verdun.
Ninety years on
they seem younger, not older,

the years between us shorter,
and the war they fought in
never-ending slaughter.

Small Factory

Ivy stipples the walls like rusted nails.
Then nettles take over,
barring the doors.

Glimpses, through broken windows,
of work tables, heavy machines,
floorboards sagging earthward –

the whole enterprise
reverting to the mineral
without a murmur.

Musk Mallow

Flower of ruins and stones, the mallow warms
to old walls, to rubble, to debris,
flourishing when other flowers cease,

in rain-filled furrows, waning sun.
Its cross-stitched embroideries
trim embankments, loop through ditches

we walk along at the edge of town.
Left by the wayside, it thrives on neglect.
Its pink flowers nod as we pass,

a last saving grace, perhaps.

THE BLUE THRESHOLD

I   *Blaue Schwelle*

You stand at the blue threshold
everything will be transformed

Light will stream through your body
down to the smallest nerve endings

You will touch the air with your fingertips,
leave an imprint gentle as pollen

You can almost live on colors alone,
the whitewashed room, the marigold window,

the stairs you climb, one by one,
in linen-blue light

You will open wide the sashes,
lean out into the September afternoon

and remember, as long as you can,
these seconds flecked with gold,

this breeze acknowledging you
as against all odds

you welcome the passing of time.

II *Common Blue*

The filigreed blue wings of *Polyammatus icarus*
hovering in morning light between the doorstep

and your rubber garden clogs make you wonder
what could be common about a butterfly

steeped in such a tender blue
as to raise your expectations

not only for the day laid out before you
with all its milky hours unfilled

but for the species itself,
despite all evidence to the contrary;

you don't know if it's indolence or ignorance
that encourages you, time after time,

to throw in your lot with the optimists,
whoever they may be, or at least

to fix your attention to this lightness
so unlike your own oscillating moods,

this flutter of blue that strings you along
over grass-tips and flowers

for as long as it remains in sight,
commanding you in its leisurely way

not to let your thoughts wander off
as they're wont to do

but to hold on as it ascends,
or so you like to think,

into the gold and dizzying air
while you reflect upon

the difference between hope
and faith, and decide,

not for the first
nor the last time,

how you will steer
your own uncertain path.

III *Raiment*

Under cover of the stars
we make up our bed

our heads at the North Star
our feet at Sagittarius

flung out to the cardinal points
we'll sleep in harmony

the roof above us
beneath a tapestry of rain

while all the dyes, plum-red and peacock-blue,
moss-green and saffron-gold,

thread into our lives
with their richest brocades

If only we could wake anew,
earth-bound souls

who must content ourselves
with the azure wings of butterflies.